Today's Superstars

Entertainment

Jessica Simpson

by Susan Mitchell

Gareth Stevens
Publishing

Please visit our web site at: www.garethstevens.com
For a free color catalog describing Gareth Stevens Publishing's
list of high-quality books, call 1-800-542-2595 (USA) or
1-800-387-3178 (Canada).

Library of Congress Cataloging-in-Publication Data

Mitchell, Susan K.
      Jessica Simpson / Susan Mitchell.
            p. cm. — (Today's superstars: entertainment)
      Includes bibliographical references and index.
      ISBN: 978-0-8368-8201-8 (lib. bdg.)
      1. Simpson, Jessica, 1980-—Juvenile literature. 2. Singers—
United States—Biography—Juvenile literature. I. Title.
ML3930.S57M58   2008
782.42164092—dc22   2007017324

This edition first published in 2008 by
Gareth Stevens Publishing
A Weekly Reader® Company
1 Reader's Digest Road
Pleasantville, NY 10570-7000 USA

Copyright © 2008 by Gareth Stevens, Inc.

Editor: Gini Holland
Art direction and design: Tammy West
Picture research: Diane Laska-Swanke
Production: Jessica Yanke

Photo credits: Cover, © Kevin Mazur/WireImage.com; pp. 5, 6, 9, 20, 22,
28 © AP Images; pp. 11, 15, 17 The Everett Collection; p. 12 © Steve
Fenn/ABC/courtesy Everett Collection; p. 16 © 20th Century Fox Film
Corp./courtesy Everett Collection; pp. 18, 23 © Erik C. Pendzich/Rex
Features, courtesy Everett Collection; p. 25 © Warner Brothers/courtesy
Everett Collection; p. 27 © Lions Gate/courtesy Everett Collection

Printed in the United States of America

1 2 3 4 5 6 7 8 9 11 10 09 08 07

Contents

Chapter 1 Sweet Charity 4

Chapter 2 Daughter of a Preacher-Man ..8

Chapter 3 Irresistible Image 13

Chapter 4 Newly Found Fame 19

Chapter 5 Big Screen Ambition 24

Time Line 29

Glossary 30

To Find Out More 31

Index 32

Chapter 1

Sweet Charity

Medical scrubs were not the kinds of fashions Jessica Simpson was used to. She was on a ten day trip to Africa with the charity Operation Smile. She arrived in Africa in October 2005. Jessica then traveled by bus from Nairobi to the small village of Nakuru in western Kenya. For Jessica, the journey was a life-changing experience. "I needed to escape," she said. "I needed to get away from life and surround myself [with] that which is good."

As the charity's spokesperson, she went beyond posing for pictures and shaking hands. Jessica got in on the action. She helped doctors evaluate more than 280 young children for surgery. She was a long way from a movie set or the recording studio. The African village had none of the modern comforts of her everyday life. "I had spiders in my bed, and I didn't even care because I was so tired," she said.

Jessica became particularly close to one eighteen-month-old child named Boke. Born with a cleft palate, Boke had been brought by her father. He had traveled over twelve hours on foot to find help for his daughter.

Jessica was moved by their story. She sat in on Boke's surgery from start to finish. When the procedure was done, Jessica handed the young girl back to her father. It was an experience that would change Jessica's life. "It's crazy," she said, "to go there to bring blessings to these kids, and they end up blessing you more."

Jessica also volunteers her time entertaining United States military troops with the United Service Organizations (USO). She performs in order to boost the spirits of those who serve in the armed forces.

Using Her Star Power

When Jessica returned from Africa, she went to speak to Congress in Washington, D.C.,

about the charity. She went with Congressman Trent Franks from Arizona and Dr. Bill Magee of Operation

Smile. She showed a serious side of herself that the public had rarely seen.

Dr. Magee said of her, "Jessica's involvement in Operation Smile has been a wonderful benefit to our organization. Her goodwill trip to Africa and her support . . . show her sincerity and selflessness in helping needy children and their families. Jessica's outer and inner beauty shine through and she is an inspiration to the thousands of kids around the world who need our help."

Fact File

In Africa, Jessica was inspired by seeing a rare double rainbow. She said that after seeing it, she listened to "Somewhere Over The Rainbow" from *The Wizard of Oz* every day.

No Smiles at Home

The return from Africa also marked another change in Jessica's life. Her three-year marriage to

One Smile at a Time

Operation Smile is a world-wide charity founded by Dr. Bill Magee and his wife. On a trip overseas in the 1980s, they saw several children with facial deformities and cleft palates. People with these facial differences usually have problems with eating and breathing. In many countries, families cannot afford surgery to fix these problems. Dr. Magee and his wife decided to start a group to help these children. The charity's volunteers travel to over thirty countries. They have done more than one hundred thousand surgeries for children and young adults. Jessica Simpson became involved with Operation Smile in 2001.

singer Nick Lachey was ending. Shortly after her return home, Jessica filed for divorce. She told one magazine that she realized her marriage was over when her husband did not go with her to Africa. "I went there on our three-year anniversary," she said. "He stayed home." Nick was actually in Sweden recording an album, but his absence hurt Jessica. "Everything became so clear. I was in hospitals with all these sick kids," she said. "I just knew I needed to find something more in my life, on my own." Her charity work opened a new chapter in her life. It brought her back to the same values she had been raised with before she became a star.

Chapter 2 — Daughter of a Preacher-Man

Jessica Ann Simpson was born on July 10, 1980, in Dallas, Texas. Her parents, Joe and Tina Simpson, were both native Texans. Her father was a Baptist preacher and her mother had been an aerobics instructor. Younger sister Ashlee was born when Jessica was four years old.

As a young girl, Jessica moved often as her father went from church to church with his ministry. In 1990, her father got a permanent job. He became the youth minister at The Heights Baptist Church in Richardson, Texas.

The Simpson family was very involved in church. Jessica's way to take part was through singing. She began performing in front of a church crowd at the age of five. It wasn't long before she began to dream of being a singer when she got older.

Not in the Club

When Jessica was twelve years old, her dance teacher took her to Dallas, Texas, for an audition for *The All New Mickey Mouse Club* television show. Jessica won the competition! She headed to Orlando, Florida, for the contest finals. While waiting to perform, she watched the performance of another contestant, Christina Aguilera. "All I can remember is watching Christina on the TV . . . and it intimidated the [heck] out of me," she said.

In her audition, Jessica completely froze. She forgot the words to her song. Jessica was not chosen for *The All New*

Mickey Mouse Club. Britney Spears and Christina Aguilera, however, both won spots on the show. This audition started Jessica's long competition with both singers.

With her family's help, Jessica was determined to work even harder. Her parents hired a vocal coach to help Jessica. She began to perform at other churches and gospel events around Texas. At one church camp, Jessica got another chance at stardom when she was thirteen years old. Gospel music producer Buster Soaries was also at the church camp. He had worked with Whitney Houston when she was young. Mr. Soaries was blown away by Jessica's talent. He signed her to his record label that same day.

It looked like Jessica's dream was finally coming true. She began recording her first gospel album. Before it could be finished, however, the record company went out of business. Jessica was heartbroken. Her father borrowed money from Jessica's grandmother to finish the album.

Fact File

When she was sixteen, Jessica played the role of Cassie in her high school's production of *A Chorus Line*.

In The House of Mouse

The Mickey Mouse Club was a very popular television show in the 1950s. It first aired in 1955 and ran until 1959. The show featured young performers called "Mouseketeers." They performed songs and danced in each episode. *The Mickey Mouse Club* was brought back in the 1970s. It was not successful, however. In the 1990s, the Disney Channel brought it back again with a new name. The *All New Mickey Mouse Club* had an updated format. It still had song and dance acts, but comedy skits were added also. The show ran from 1989 to 1994 with reruns through May of 1996.

Stars like Justin Timberlake (*top right*), Christina Aguilera (*middle right*), and Britney Spears (*bottom right*) started their careers on *The All New Mickey Mouse Club.*

Jessica performed her new single, "I Belong to Me" on the television talk show, *The View*. Host Rosie O'Donnell personally chose Jessica Simpson to be her first guest when she joined the show.

As time went by, Jessica decided to cross over to more mainstream pop music. Jessica's parents hired a lawyer to represent her. In 1997, the lawyer got Jessica a meeting with a top executive at Columbia Records. The executive was very impressed. She asked Jessica to travel to New York and meet with the head of Columbia Records, Tommy Mottola. This was the chance Jessica and her family had worked so hard for.

Fact File

Jessica was elected Homecoming Queen twice at J.J. Pearce High School in Richardson, Texas.

Irresistible Image

Chapter 3

After Jessica's Columbia Records audition, Mr. Mottola asked her to sit down. He asked her what she wanted to do with her music. Jessica said she wanted to be an example to other young girls. Her answer impressed Mr. Mottola and so did her singing. He signed her to a four-album contract that day.

It took more than two years before Jessica's first album was released. To make things more frustrating for Jessica, both Britney Spears and Christina Aguilera had albums released before her. Both had signed record deals at the same time as Jessica. Jessica felt as if she were in third place behind these two stars again. But she

Making Music Makers

Tommy Mottola is one of the most successful recording executives in history. He was born in 1949 in the Bronx, New York. He grew up wanting a singing career of his own. When that did not happen, Mottola started a career managing musicians.

By working his way up through the company, Mottola eventually became the president of Sony Music. By then, he was one of the most powerful men in music. He also met his future wife through his job. One day, he heard the demo tape of Mariah Carey. He signed her to a singing contract and the two eventually married. They divorced, however, in 1998.

knew she couldn't let that get her down. She just had to keep singing and trying to do her best.

In April of 1999, Jessica was the opening act for the boy band, 98 Degrees. One of the band members was Nick Lachey. Nick and Jessica had begun dating earlier that same year.

Sweet Kisses, her first album, was released in November 1999. Jessica's star was on the rise and as usual, her family was there to help. Her father became

Fact File

Due to her singing tour, Jessica was unable to complete high school. She finished her credits by mail and received a GED in August 1997.

Jessica sported a mini skirt when she sang in 2000 at Music Mania. She believes it's possible to dress in fun and attractive ways while staying true to good moral values.

her full-time manager. Jessica's mother handled the fashion. Ashlee was one of Jessica's dancers.

Not So Sweet Anymore

While *Sweet Kisses* had sold well, it did not do as well as albums by Christina Aguilera and Britney Spears. The record company executives decided that Jessica needed to make some changes to her image for her second album. They wanted her to be more daring in the way she dressed.

They also wanted her to lose weight. This whole image change made Jessica uncomfortable. The final change in Jessica's life at this point was a break up with her boyfriend, Nick. By the time her second album, *Irresistible*, was released in May 2001, Jessica's entire world had changed.

All An Act

Although Jessica started out feeling uncomfortable about changing her image, she soon saw her image as just an act. Soon, she felt free to look at real acting roles. By 2002, Jessica had a guest role on television's *That 70's Show*.

The year 2002 brought more than just career changes to Jessica's life. Nick and

Fact File

Jessica played California golden girl Annette on *That 70's Show*. She played a love interest of Ashton Kutcher's character, Kelso.

Jessica had gotten back together in late 2001. On February 10, 2002, Nick asked Jessica to marry him. Most people in the music industry, including Jessica's father, thought the two were making a huge mistake.

This time, Jessica decided to go with her heart. On October 26, 2002, Jessica and Nick were married in Austin, Texas. The spent their honeymoon in Fiji. When they came back, Nick and Jessica moved into a two-million-dollar home. They also had an interesting proposal from Joe that would change both of their lives.

Jessica acts with Nick Lachey on their MTV show *Newlyweds.* MTV originally wanted to make a reality show about Nick and Jessica's wedding. But *InStyle* magazine got that idea first, so MTV decided to create the *Newlyweds* show instead.

More Than Precious Metals

The Recording Industry Association of America (RIAA) is the organization that has certified albums Gold or Platinum since 1958. Albums can also reach Multi-Platinum or Diamond certifications. The certifications are given based on the number of albums sold.

Gold albums have sold 500,000 copies. An album is certified Platinum if it sells one million copies. If an album sells several million copies, it is called Multi-Platinum. In 1999, the RIAA created the Diamond certification for albums that have sold more than ten million copies.

Jessica has three gold certified albums and two multi-platinum certified albums. Here, she shows off her *In This Skin* Gold Disk award.

Newly Found Fame

Although Jessica's father had been against the wedding, he now presented the idea of a reality show based on her marriage. The show would be called *Newlyweds* and air on MTV. Both Nick and Jessica were unsure about the idea. Television crews and cameras would be watching their every move. They would be listening to all their conversations.

Joe Simpson believed it would be a great tool to promote Jessica's upcoming albums. In the end, Nick and Jessica agreed. *Newlyweds'* first episode aired in the summer of 2003. It was an instant hit! Jessica's third album, *In This Skin*, was released at the same time. At first, the

Nick and Jessica first met in 1998 at the Hollywood Christmas Parade. Just weeks after seeing her, Nick told 98 Degrees band members, "I'm going to marry that girl."

Fact File

Newlyweds was originally developed for Michael Jackson and Lisa Marie Presley.

Newlyweds show did not help Jessica's album sales.

With the TV show, Jessica once again had an image makeover. She became famous for her "dumb" personality. On *Newlyweds*, Jessica often said weird things that made her seem less than smart. In one famous episode, she asks Nick if Chicken of the Sea is made of chicken or fish. It is canned tuna. In another episode, she wonders if buffalo wings are made of buffalo.

Newlyweds was a "reality" show in which the camera followed the famous couple around in real life. Critics of the show claimed that the show did not give a true picture of Nick and Jessica. Nick was shown as the patient husband, but sometimes he seemed too critical. Jessica was shown as a ditzy slob who shopped way too much. But this was not an image that Jessica had a problem with. She liked it much better than the super-slim, daringly dressed image she had to take on before.

98 Degrees of Cool

Nick Lachey's home life and upbringing were very different from Jessica's. He was born in Kentucky in 1973, but grew up in Ohio. His parents were divorced and he has a brother, Drew. While their backgrounds are different, Nick and Jessica's career beginnings were very similar.

Just as Jessica seemed to follow behind Christina Aguilera and Britney Spears, Nick had his share of coming in behind the leaders. His band, 98 Degrees, was formed with Nick, his brother Drew, and two of their friends. Their first album was released in 1997. 98 Degrees consistently came in behind the popular boy-bands, *NSYNC and the Backstreet Boys. Nick experienced the same frustration that Jessica had.

When Nick decided to pursue a solo career, 98 Degrees never officially broke up. In October 2006, Nick hinted they might record another album together.

For Better or Worse?

Jessica proved that getting married was not a career killer. She had never been more popular. Jessica began to get offers to appear in commercials. She starred in commercials for Pizza Hut, Ice Breakers mints, and Proactiv acne products.

In April 2004, Nick and Jessica starred in their own television special. The *Nick and Jessica Variety Hour* featured the couple singing and acting in comedy skits. The second season of *Newlyweds* began in 2004 also. It was more popular than ever.

Finally, the impact of the *Newlyweds* show started to increase Jessica's album sales. Jessica's record company re-released *In This Skin*. It began climbing the charts! The album ended up selling more copies than any of her previous records.

The success Jessica gained from the TV show did come with a price. The marriage she and Nick let television viewers watch was slowly crumbling. While Jessica's star was on the rise, Nick's had stayed put. *Newlyweds* had not helped Nick's album sales. It did not seem to help his relationship with his wife, either. Nick seemed to feel he could not compete with Jessica's fame. The couple's problems were made even worse when Jessica began to get movie roles. Her rise to fame, however, was only beginning.

Fact File

On *Newlyweds*, Jessica often mangled the English language. In one episode, she thought the word platypus was pronounced "platymapus."

Sing It, Sister

One of Jessica's biggest fans has always been her younger sister Ashlee. She got her start dancing during Jessica's concert tours. Since then, Ashlee has launched a singing career of her own. With more of a rock-star image, she has tried to be seen as the exact opposite of Jessica.

Her debut album, *Autobiography*, was released in July 2004. She is also managed by her father, Joe. Ashlee has struggled with her singing reputation after she was caught lip-synching on an episode of *Saturday Night Live*.

Ashlee Simpson got her acting start before Jessica. In 2002, she got a recurring role on the television show *7th Heaven*. Here, in May 2004, she poses with Jessica.

Fact File

Jessica once said her favorite childhood memory was of Ashlee being born.

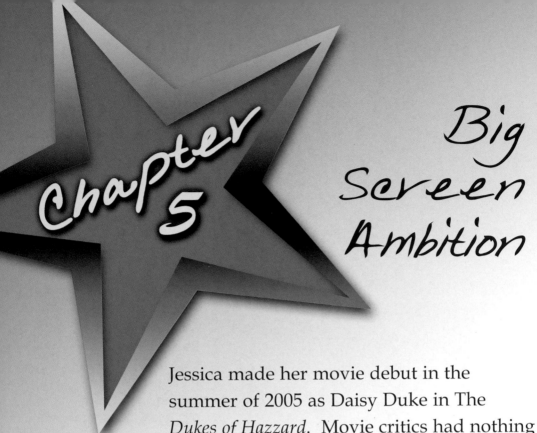

Chapter 5

Big Screen Ambition

Jessica made her movie debut in the summer of 2005 as Daisy Duke in The *Dukes of Hazzard*. Movie critics had nothing good to say about Jessica's acting. But while most critics hated the movie, fans disagreed. It was the number one movie at the box office when it was released.

Jessica recorded a song for the movie as well. "These Boots Are Made for Walkin'" was originally sung in the 1960s by Nancy Sinatra. Jessica re-recorded it for the movie. She also shot a video for the song that was banned in many countries. Many thought it was much too racy.

Her role in *The Dukes of Hazzard* had meant long periods of time away from

Jessica listens on the set of *The Dukes of Hazard*. During the filming of this movie, Jessica was upset about rumors that she was romantically involved with co-star Johnny Knoxville (*far right*).

Nick. By the end of 2005, after her trip to Africa, Jessica filed for divorce. The divorce was finalized in June of 2006. The couple who had rocketed to stardom with their televised marriage had split in less than three years.

To work through her feelings, Jessica headed back to the recording studio. She started working on her fourth album. *A Public Affair* was released in August 2006. The album did not do well on the record charts and sold less than a million copies.

Jessica also had a supporting role in her second movie that same year. *Employee of the Month* opened in movie theaters in October 2006. Jessica played a cashier at a discount store. In the movie, she is being romanced by fellow

Fact File

Jessica beat out Britney Spears for the role of Daisy Duke.

Hot Enough to Melt

Jessica was honored when she was chosen to have a wax statue of herself placed in New York's Madame Tussaud's Wax Museum. Now, her statue stands with those of many other superstars.

Marie Tussaud started the famous museum in the 1800s. She learned how to make wax models from her employer. When he died, he left all of his wax figures to Marie. Many were of famous historical figures. Marie Tussaud moved to London, England in 1802. She traveled with her wax models and displayed them for the public to see.

Today, the main Madame Tussaud's Wax Museum is located in London, England. Other Madame Tussaud's Museums display wax figures in major cities all over the world. Jessica Simpson is just one of hundreds of stars who have had their images preserved in wax.

workers. The movie did relatively well at the box office. Critics, however, blasted Jessica's acting once again. If it bothered her, she didn't let it show.

The bad reviews also did not stop Jessica from getting more movie roles. Her third movie, *Blonde Ambition*, is scheduled to be released in 2007. It will be Jessica's first starring role. "I've never had the leading role," said Jessica, "and with this one it's really going to be nice to just dive in and wrap my arms around it."

Stepping Stones

As with all of her acting jobs, Jessica will tie her album into the *Blonde Ambition* project. For

this movie, she will re-release a track from her *A Public Affair* album. Jessica also has a starring role in the upcoming film, *The Witness*. Filming of the movie was scheduled to begin in March 2007.

Jessica's career and image continue to change. With the help of her family, she keeps reaching her goals. At the age of twenty-seven, she has accomplished many of the things she has set out to do. Her future as a rising star looks successful as well. "Honestly, I want to continue climbing," said Jessica. "I never want to reach the top. Because, then what … you tumble down? I don't want to do that. I want to continue life climbing."

Jessica starred in *Employee of the Month* with Dax Shepard (*left*) and comedian Dane Cook (*right*).

Fact File

Jessica has a pet Malti-poo named Daisy. She is part Maltese and part poodle.

A Head for Business

Over the years, Jessica has used her name and talent to succeed in business as well as entertainment. In 2004, Jessica launched a line of edible beauty products. Because they are edible — and tasty — she named her cosmetics line Dessert.

In the fashion world, she and her mother created a line of clothing. She based the designs of much of the clothing on the character Daisy Duke. Jessica has also loaned her name to a line of shoes. In 2006, she helped launch a line of wigs and hair extensions with her hairstylist and good friend, Ken Paves.

In 2005, Jessica promoted Dessert Cosmetics. In 2006, Jessica was sued by the clothing company that produces her JS and Princy clothing brands. They claimed that she failed to wear or promote the clothing lines.

Time Line

1980   Jessica Simpson is born in Dallas, Texas

1997   Signs a four-album recording contract with Tommy Mottola.

1998   Goes on tour opening for 98 Degrees; begins dating Nick Lachey.

1999   First album, *Sweet Kisses*, is released.

2001   *Irresistible* is released; Jessica and Nick briefly break up.

2002   Gets first TV role in *That 70s Show*; marries Nick.

2003   *Newlyweds* debuts on MTV; *In This Skin*, her third album, is released.

2004   *In This Skin* is re-released and sales soar; launches Dessert cosmetics.

2005   Plays Daisy Duke in *The Dukes of Hazzard* movie; divorces Nick Lachey.

2006   Has supporting role in the movie *Employee of the Month*; launches HairDo.

2007   Finishes shooting movie, *The Witness*; has first starring role in *Blonde Ambition*.

Glossary

audition — in entertainment, a test of a singer or actor's abilities

certified — confirmed to meet certain standards, such as number of records sold

charity — an organization that donates time, money, or services to those in need

cleft palate — birth defect where the roof of the mouth is not properly formed

critics — in entertainment, people whose job is to give their opinions about movies, TV shows, or music

debut — the first appearance or release of something, such as a movie or album release

demo tape — a recording that singers send to record companies to try to get discovered

image — the way a person is viewed by the public.

lip-synching — to move one's lips to a recorded song without actually singing

mainstream — popularly accepted by many people

reality show — a minimally scripted TV show that shows real people in real situations

spokesperson — someone who represents an organization or company

vocal coach — an expert who helps someone learn to sing better

To Find Out More

Books
Jessica Simpson. Real-Life Reader Biography (series).
John Bankston (Mitchell Lane Publishers)

Jessica Simpson and Nick Lachey. People in the News
(series). Terri Dougherty (Lucent Books)

Videos
Jessica Simpson – Reality Tour Live (Sony)

Newlyweds – Seasons 1-4 (Paramount Home Video)

Web Sites
Jessica Simpson
www.jessicasimpson.com
Official Web site.

Newlyweds
*www.mtv.com/ontv/dyn/newlyweds-nick_and_jessica/
series.jhtml*
MTV website for the TV show.

Publisher's note to educators and parents: Our editors have carefully
reviewed these Web sites to ensure that they are suitable for children.
Many Web sites change frequently, however, and we cannot guarantee
that a site's future contents will continue to meet our high standards
of quality and educational value. Be advised that children should be
closely supervised whenever they access the Internet.

Index

98 Degrees 14, 20, 21

A Public Affair 25, 27
Africa 4, 5, 6, 7, 25
Aguilera, Christina
   9, 10, 11, 13, 15, 21
*All New Mickey
   Mouse Club, The* 9,
   10, 11
Ashton, Kutcher 16

Backstreet Boys 21
Blonde Ambition
   26, 27

Columbia Records 12

Dessert Cosmetics 28
*Dukes of Hazzard,
   The* 24, 25

*Employee of the
   Month* 25, 27

Franks, Congressman
   Trent 6

Houston, Whitney 10

In This Skin 18, 19, 22
InStyle magazine 17
Irresistible 16

Knight, Gladys 22

Lachey, Nick 7, 9,
   14, 16, 17, 19, 20,
   21, 22, 25

Madame Tussaud's
   Wax Museum 26
Magee, Dr. Bill 6, 7
*Mickey Mouse Club,
   The* 11
Mottola, Tommy 12,
   13, 14

Newlyweds 17, 19,
   20, 21, 22
*Nick and Jessica
   Variety Hour,
   The* 21

Operation Smile 4, 5,
   6, 7

Paves, Ken 28

RIAA 18

Simpson, Ashlee 8, 9,
   15, 23
Simpson, Joe 8, 9, 14,
   17, 19, 23
Simpson, Tina 8,
   9, 15
Soaries, Buster 10
Spears, Britney 10,
   11, 13, 15, 21, 25
Sweet Kisses 14, 15

That 70's Show 16
"These Boots Are
   Made For Walkin'"
   24
Timberlake, Justin 11

USO 5

Witness, The 27

About the Author

Susan K. Mitchell has always loved books, movies and music. She is a preschool teacher and author of several children's picture books. Susan has also written many non-fiction chapter books for kids. She lives near Houston, Texas with her husband, two daughters, a dog, and two cats. She dedicates this book to Carrie, who appreciates her humor.